SONGWRITING - is truly a gift...
... an *AWESOME* and SPECIAL
...Blessing to the Writer!!

Writing Songs for any type of music is an extraordinary gift that can come only from God. To watch a song begin in its simplest form and develop right before your eyes shows even the largest skeptic of the great gift that is bestowed to the many talented songwriters!

It is one thing to write something and an entirely different notion to see what it can become in the final product. It is *this process* that can be studied as a craft. It is *this gift* that is almost unexplainable.

If I were to ask you, 'How can a writer write?' what do you think your answer would be? How can the singer sing? Or even, how can a dancer or musician feel the music? How can an interior decorator picture something on a wall, in their mind, that is not already there?

We all have gifts; that is undeniable. I believe with all my heart that our gifts, no matter how large or small they seem, come from God. Our problem lies in answering the age-old question, "What do we do with them?"

Do you think we should leave them at home when we go places? Do you think we should ignore them? Do you think we should leave them untested?

I hope you will never underestimate the gift you have just because you haven't used it. There is a tremendous difference between the man who won't do it and the man who just hasn't tried it yet.

Why would a man who fails want to continue trying? The answer is… it is because he knows and believes that he could be just…

ONE ATTEMPT AWAY FROM SUCCESS!!

That line of thinking is what drives every artist in the world. The greatest failure would be to the man who never tries!!

Attempting to write a *great song* should be every *want-to-be-songwriter*'s desire. The degree of your success and accomplishments will vary. You must never stop… never yield… never wane…

You must set yourself up for success!! If you plan for it, look for it, and desire it, who knows; you might just get it!!

The fact is, you can learn the process of songwriting no matter how far you test your talents. It doesn't matter really. As you begin the study, you will find yourself many times paying extra special attention to the song playing meagerly and quietly in the background while at the mall. You will then ask yourself the question, "Has this mall always played songs while we shopped and perhaps I just haven't noticed? I wonder.. Who is the artist singing that song? Which line was the hook?" Soon you find yourself humming along as you recognize the tune and lyrics.

Suddenly you realize you have been singing along under your breath because you, too, love certain catchy phrases that have stuck out in your mind subconsciously through the years.

Again, this is a process; a process that works in all genres of music. It will work for Country Music! It will work for you!

Now, read on and have a wonderful time learning…

TABLE *of* CONTENTS

Writing Songs

the Introduction

When I think of Country Music... immediately Hank Williams comes to mind. Suddenly other names flood my mind; names like George Jones, Tammy Wynette, Loretta Lynn, Willie Nelson, Waylon Jennings, Glen Campbell, and many, many more. The legacy of Hank Williams and the era it all ushered in changed the stage for Country Music forever. Notice I said 'changed' and not 'set'.

I wasn't around when it began. Neither was he. Actually, Hank Williams helped to usher in 'Honky Tonk', just another sub-genre of the Country Music craze.

So, when did it begin? Who were some of the main players? Does it really matter?

Hey, just one question at a time... will ya?! Or better said, just one answer at a time!!

Sure it matters! Artists very well *better* know what they like and what their audience likes to hear them sing. Every singer has a gift and a certain sound.

Likewise, every writer has a gift and a certain style of writing. Sometimes their gift is so huge that they can write many, many different styles. That will be tested through time. In the beginning, the writer should not worry about knowing what their gift is or what it encompasses. It is much more important that the writer just recognize that they have a gift. God does the rest as we use our gifts.

Now to reiterate... It is very, very important for a writer to dig deep into the history and culture of where they consider themselves to work and operate. Much of that will come out and begin to shine in the personality of the writer as he or she begins to write. Without even realizing it, they 'find' themselves. As they begin to turn out songs, so will a certain style develop and be set. Don't dwell on it; just DO IT! Study... Learn... Write!!

A Little HISTORY

According to <u>Wikipedia</u>, '**Country music** is a popular American musical style that began in the rural Southern United States in the 1920s. It takes its roots from Western cowboy and folk music. Country music often consists of ballads and dance tunes with generally simple forms and harmonies accompanied by mostly string instruments such as banjoes, electric and acoustic guitars, fiddles such as violins, and harmonicas.'

The online encyclopedia also states, 'The term *country music* gained popularity in the 1940s in preference to the earlier term *hillbilly music*. The term *country music* is used today to describe many styles and subgenres. In 2009 Country music was the most listened to rush hour radio genre during the evening commute, and second most popular in the morning commute.

Apparently the early Scottish settlers enjoyed the fiddle because it could be played to sound sad and mournful or bright and bouncy. The fiddle, the German derived dulcimer, the Italian mandolin, the Spanish guitar, and the West African banjo were the most common musical instruments.

Even today, these early instruments that had made their way in the pioneering American era still help to push the recognized sounds of Country Music.

Country Music was introduced as a Southern phenomenon. In the South, folk music was a combination of cultural strains, combining musical traditions of a variety of ethnic groups in the region. Some instrumental songs and tunes from British and Irish immigrants were the basis of folk songs and ballads that form what is now known as 'old time music', from which Country Music descended.

Many blacks and whites in rural communities in the south often worked and played together. So, it could be said that Country Music was created by African-Americans and European-Americans alike.

The 1920s

The first commercial recordings of what was considered country music were "Arkansas Traveler" and "Turkey in the Straw" by fiddlers Henry Gilliland & A.C. (Eck) Robertson on June 30, 1925 for Victor Records; although Columbia Records began issuing records with that 'hillbilly' music in 1924.

Notable names like Fiddlin' John Carson and Vernon Dalhart began turning out records. Hillbilly musicians like Cliff Carlisle came on the scene. Also, in the 1920's, the steel guitar was introduced to the Americas from Hawaii.

Jimmie Rodgers and the Carter Family made huge leaps in the industry. Rodgers fused hillbilly country, gospel, jazz, blues, pop, cowboy, and folk; and many of his best songs were his compositions, including "Blue Yodel", which sold over a million records and established Rodgers as the premier singer of early country music. For the next 17 years, beginning in 1927, the Carters recorded some 300 old-time ballads, traditional tunes, country songs and gospel hymns; these were all representative of America's southeastern heritage and folklore.

Adding to all of this hoopla was the introduction of the Grand Ole Opry in 1925 in Nashville, TN. It was the radio station of WSM-AM that seemed to push these sounds across airwaves everywhere. Early stars were Uncle Dave Macon and Roy Acuff. The station later went to 50,000 watts and it was WSM's signal that could be heard almost clean across the country… or so it seemed.

The 1930s

Because of the 1920s, songs that had become popular on the vinyl record had now made their way to the big screen. Hollywood had begun to make movies which included cowboy songs, or Western music. These popular singing cowboys from the era included names like Roy Rogers, the Sons of the Pioneers, and Gene Autry.

Then came the singing cowgirls. Patsy Montana became popular and opened the door for female artists everywhere with her history making song "I Want To Be a Cowboy's Sweetheart".

Another country musician who had become very popular as the leader of a "hot string band," and who also appeared in Hollywood Westerns, was Bob Wills. Bob's mix of jazz and country, which started out as dance hall music, would soon be labeled as Western swing. Tex Williams and Spade Cooley also had very popular bands and appeared in films. Western swing, at its peak, rivaled the popularity of other big band jazz.

The boogie became known and so did artists like Tennessee Ernie Ford and Arthur Smith.

The 1940s

After WWII, there emerged a group that helped to usher in Bluegrass, Gospel, and Folk in a way it had never been seen before. The group was called 'Bluegrass' and it included none other than Bill Monroe along with Lester Flatt and Earl Scruggs. It was Roy Acuff who introduced them on the stage of the Grand Ole Opry for the first time.

It was then that the Honky Tonk was introduced which brought to light artists like Ernest Tubb, Kitty Wells, and yes, then my previously mention of Hank Williams. But you see, It didn't stop there. Soon to follow was the likes of names like Jerry Lee Lewis, Chuck Berry, and the incomparable Elvis Presley. Also emerging were other large names like George Jones and Webb Pierce. It was Webb Pierce who had 13 singles at number one for 113 weeks and who charted 48 songs during the decade of the 1950s. Of those, 31 reached the 'Top 10' and 26 landed in the top four.

Elvis Presley was joined by Johnny Cash and Carl Perkins to own the number two, three, and four spots on the Billboard charts at one time. It could never be argued against the prominence of Country Music, or some sub genre of it, after that.

Present Day

The Country Music as we know it still had some evolving to do. From the likes of Loretta Lynn, Jim Reeves, and Tammy Wynette to the truly different sounds of Patsy Cline, Country had made its mark on the music industry. In 1962, the world even saw the introduction of a blind, black man who would add a popular soul-country cross-over by the name of Ray Charles.

Other artists evolved in an even stranger genre… Outlaw Country! Willie Nelson, Hank Williams, Jr., Waylon Jennings, and David Alan Coe were just some in this category.

Seemingly, there were these eccentric artists and then there were the normal. But even then, the word normal can't be used too casual.

Country pop evolved which issued the likes of Glen Campbell, Bobbie Gentry, Anne Murray, John Denver, B. J. Thomas, Olivia Newton-John, and Marie Osmond. Even Linda Ronstadt and The Bellamy Brothers joined in.

From Charlie Rich and Dolly Parton to Kenny Rogers, Crystal Gayle, Ronnie Milsap, and Barbara Mandrell… yes the list had grown even bigger and such was the stage of the Country Music scene.

Why Is This All Important?

A person's heritage goes much deeper than the color of the skin. The color is just an adaptation between the heritage and culture of one's past and the climate and surroundings the body is subjected to. Things evolve… so does our bodies… so does the music.

It is immensely important to understand how something has evolved to begin to see how we fit into the picture. Our hopes and dreams all rest in the basic understanding of the things we hope to produce. This fundamental groundwork showcases, if for no other reason, certain artists and sounds of their music.

As you begin to write, you will see how important it is to recognize the 'sound' and 'feel' your song is trying to take on. Let me say that in another way. As you craft a song, the song begins to take on its own personality.

You can influence it somewhat by how you write it. But make no mistake...!! You do not have full control. You're the writer, but God is the giver of the gift. As you use the gift, you do have the ability to change it in any way you want. However, you will begin to notice that some places certain lines fit better than others. You will see that depending upon the wording and phrasing, the song's 'sound' might need to be speeded up or slowed down. That's a funny thing. You're the writer... You're the creator... But now, it has a 'MIND', so to speak, of its own!!

The more you learn about the craft, the more you will be able to have the song end up like you want it to. Understand that if you see information repeated, don't think that the book was a waste of money. The material might just be THAT IMPORTANT!!

Study it! Learn it! Eat it! Sleep with it! In the end... JUST DO IT!!

Major Components or Factors
Of the Country Music Song

Style

Sound

Exploit People's Passions

Going Against the Apparent 'Norm'

Touch Everyone's Emotions

Appeal to Every Race and Nationality

Appeal to Every Age Group

Set the Appropriate Tone for Certain Occasions

Non-Offensive

Biblical Correctness

Dance-Ability Factor

Style

The style of a song would lend itself toward any type of song you can craft. There are listeners in every genre of music and plenty of people to appreciate and enjoy almost every performer. However, where there are performers, there are ratings, charts, etc... There is an old saying… 'Dance to the Fiddler who 'brung' you'. In other words, the styles of the past and present would definitely be worth imitating and studying. Those are the styles that have sold millions of records.

Let this sink in. A good song is a good song; no matter the genre. However, a song's popularity, which ultimately determines the 'Hit Song' is not necessarily a result of the best written song. The same could be said of the style.

There is no way to 'turn history back' and see what would have happened if a different artist had first performed a song or if the same artist had changed the beat or feel of the same song. If only someone could release it with multiple performers and see which version creates the most 'hype'. Although that could be done, no one could still say what it would have been like to have released only the 'one' version with 'one' artist and to see it as compared to an alternative. You see, once a song has become popular, or not, coming out with it a second time just picks up where the first group's popularity with the song left off.

There have been artists that have re-cut other's songs. Still, they were playing off the popularity of the first. It was an intentional attempt to grab the likeability of the first song that had already come about in the marketplace. If the music industry loves 'Song A', then your fans just might like it if you were to come out with it too.

The better the writer can pinpoint a correct style and 'feel' of the song as he/she is writing it, the better everything gels when it comes time to launch and pitch it.

The style definitely determines the song's acceptability and where it will go.

Pitched to the wrong artists

Or artists with a different style of singing
The song is already dead

Also, keep in mind that a song will become a 'Bigger Hit' if it is more inclusive than exclusive. Some songs, or styles of songs, tend to be loved by some and despised by others while other songs are accepted across genre lines.

Example… Although many people love Rap Music, many music lovers who prefer songs with more of a 'Melody' do not like Rap songs. Therefore, although a song may be a really big hit with Rap, it may be dead within other genres.

Rappers, and their fans, probably hate 'twangy' songs like Patsy Cline sang.

A love song, on the other hand, may be accepted by Country Music lovers, Gospel Music lovers, Rap Music lovers, etc… and rejected by none. So, naturally, a 'Hit Song' in that realm would be even a bigger hit!

Sound

There is a very distinct and certain predictable sound that the Country Music song has. That predictable sound is... 'Anything'!! Yes, that's right! We have already studied the diversity of Country Music. This is probably the most diverse segment of music overall because it encompasses almost every other genre in some way that you can imagine.

From Gospel music to soul, Country Music has some artist who has blazed a raw trail and already set precedence for a particular style of music. That actually is a good thing.

People's appreciation for music has expanded and their minds are open. They are used to many diverse cultures in almost any country now. From the many different religions to the many different styles of dress, the world pretty much will accept everything at least somewhere in some city and in some segment of the market.

The predictable concept of the sound being 'Unpredictable' is so true. The most accepted styles still will go along with our teaching about going with what is selling now and has in the past. If they loved Elvis, they will love his style of songs still. If they loved George Jones, then they will love other songs that are similar. Honky Tonk is in. And, as long as people have troubles in their life, they want to 'sing' their troubles away and get close to other people having those same troubles who can identify with them.

Exploit People's Passions

Country Music has embraced so many varied types of music that it accepts most any conceivable notion. The problem is really the airwaves. The FCC has certain restrictions on public performances and that is probably what has held the industry back.

Already profanity, if mildly used, is slightly tolerated. Suggestive themes are even allowed under mild terms. I'm really not sure what is allowed and refused anymore.

Still, a smart writer would want to examine and try to understand his or her own values and write accordingly.

If you were wanting to hit the Honky Tonk sound, there are plenty of Bars and Bar-Patrons ready and willing to listen to your song exploiting their excessive 'Passion' for drinking.

David Allen Coe once sang a song called 'You Never Even Call Me by my Name'. Inside the song, there is a small recitation giving reference that he was wanting to make it the 'Perfect' Country Music song. But, he says...

"Well, a friend of mine named Steve Goodman wrote that song...

And he told me it was the perfect Country and Western Song...

I wrote him back and I told him it was not the perfect Country and Western Song...

Because it hadn't said anything at all about... Mama... or Trains... or Prison... or Getting Drunk...

Well he sat down and wrote another verse to the song and he sent it to me...

And after reading it I realized that my friend had written the perfect Country and Western Song..."

Here's how the last verse went...

Well I was drunk the day my mom got out of prison

And I went to pick her up in the rain

But before I could get to the station in my pickup truck

She got runned over by a damned old train

The song was extremely popular! That attempt to Exploit People's Passions
went over like wildfire and the crowd loved it! Understandably, however,
you probably would NOT want to sing it for your preacher at the Sunday
Lunch table!

Pulling something this extreme off is NOT advisable. It stamps you and gives
you recognition for this type of songs. Then, you will NOT be accepted as
easily by the more conservatives that you also will want to embrace. Again,
it is all up to you… You're the writer!

Just learn… *Don't Burn Bridges with <u>your</u> fans*! If they wouldn't approve of
the lyrics, then avoid it!

Going Against the Apparent 'Norm'

'Norms' are just that… the normal. Country Music is probably the most diverse type of music, as I have stated earlier. That is because so many different types of music and artists were either 'born' inside this realm or came through here.

If you were going to 'Go Against the Norm', this is the right segment to do it! The problem is… you might just alienate yourself with both YOUR fans and music lovers in general. As stated before, there is some group of people somewhere to enjoy your music.

You will come to a crossroads, if you will. Somewhere, sometime, you will approach a time where you will decide how far your style of writing varies. That is all up to you.

I would advise to simply study the 'Norm' first before deciding to do something 'crazy' or 'stupid'. Remember; it could be like a boomerang and come back to hit you!

Touch Everyone's Emotions

A Country Music Song has an implied 'must' to touch and stir the soul of the listener in ways even he or she can't imagine. With Gospel, it is more about the message. With Rap, it seems as much about how well the rapper syncopates the beat.

With Country Music, there seems to always be a superb 'Hook Line' that tickles a nerve in the listener. It might be something good, or even perhaps something they hate. But, if told in a way that they had never thought about, the listener might perk up and say, "I didn't know others thought that same way too!"

Through unique techniques, the writer can subtly suggest a word or tone through sentiments that the listener can identify with and hit a huge home run and make a lifelong fan. Many times the listener can't remember the songwriter; but they sure DO remember the song.

For example... In the section 'Exploit People's Emotions' that we have just covered and in the discussion of the song by David Allen Coe, I will had to admit that I thought that Waylon Jennings wrote the song. I didn't even remember the title of the song. I had to look it up on the computer. What I did remember was the recitation part where he said he wanted to write a 'Perfect Country and Western Song' and then he sang the last verse that mentioned 'I was drunk the day my mom got out of prison' - 'pickup truck' - '...being runned over by a (curse word) old train!' It was hard to get those inferences out of my mind.

The more someone's emotions are tapped, the better the song is remembered days, months, and even years down the road.

Life, and the choices it brings, creates good and bad days for us all. Single people have good and bad days... Married people have good and bad days... Tall people have good and bad days... People listening to Soul Gospel have good and bad days... People listening to Rock and Roll have good and bad days....

My point is that if EVERYONE in the world has undeniably good and bad days, then tapping that emotion in a song can take you on extreme lows (when we as the writer remind them of how bad it is), and then we, as the writer in the last verse perhaps, take them to the extreme highs (by letting them get a glimpse of what can improve for them!) It simply makes is a ready-made vehicle setting the stage for emotions that are definitely vulnerable.

In the Gospel Music world, we as the writers can feel great about delivering such a life-changing positive message; something right the opposite of what the normal world has to offer them.

In other songs, like Pop, Rock, it might be the 'beat' of the song that helps to liven up someone's morning.

Don't hesitate to attempt tapping into the very emotions that drive our soul. It will usually make your writing better.

Appeal to Every Race and Nationality

People want to be drawn to your music; to your song. They want to feel glad and happy to have heard the song. Alienating someone with your song is a very big 'NO - NO'. Again, a negative impact is like a disaster recovery unit at your home after a flood or tornado. The larger the explosion, the larger the cleanup operation will require. Truly recovering from some disasters are virtually impossible.

Look at it like this. One of the reasons that people are so sensitive about their race and/or nationality is that they had no say in the matter! That's right; they didn't pick their skin color. They also didn't pick where they were born. Their heritage did that, but they didn't. Some people love it; some people resent it; *BUT ALL HAVE IT*!!... Whatever our heritage is, it comes on a very individual basis.

Appeal to Every Age Group

The style and beat of a song may not appeal to everyone. Here is where you make decisions and must realize that every song is different. Each song has its own personality!

It is a good thing to try to make it appeal to as many as possible. But, it is better to make it appeal to as many as possible while making it REJECTED by as few as possible!!

Sometimes people just want to leave the concert early. If they are leaving because of negative thoughts or vibes, then it simply isn't good.

If most says it is a hit, then it probably will be a hit. Just simply try to be INCLUSIVE and resist the EXCLUSIVE ideology. Start training your mind to think about how you can say a phrase to 'include' more people and also in such a way as to not 'offend' anyone. It truly is a mindset and way of thinking.

I once thought that older people just didn't like loud and upbeat songs. Through the years, I have learned that even older people love to clap and get into the songs and feel 'alive' just like the younger. There appears to be a 'Threshold' of volume where they won't tolerate it. Anything under that 'Threshold' is okay. The volume level is up to the artist anyway, not the writer.

So, I had a bad assumption for years. Okay, I admit it. I was WRONG!! I have since learned a little more. Realizing that threshold though, as an artist, it would be smart to perform somewhere just right underneath that maximum threshold level. With writing, it applies the same. Don't make people leave your concerts because they have an extreme displeasure; rather make anyone who doesn't care for that certain song be willing to at least endure it because it isn't too offensive and be willing to wait for the next one.

Write smart!!

Set the Appropriate Tone
for Certain Occasions

Setting the Appropriate Tone for an occasion or certain type of ceremony or service is a big and important task for a writer.

Every ceremony or service has a tone that is set; even if the leader doesn't intend it to go that way or is even aware it is happening. It can be purposeful and vibrant or subtle and gentle. Sometimes a quiet worshipful mood is needed. Perhaps it is an upbeat type of event that needs a little more lively music.

Special Occasion songs can set the tone for certain events. These can range from Christenings to celebrations and from funerals to weddings. It is easy to see how certain songs are selected for these events

As a writer, I find it fun to write something different from my norm every once in a while. A change-up does me good like medicine for the soul.

Writing a theme song is normally pretty hard. It is a specific type of song with a specific intended message; depending upon the type of theme song you are writing. A Gospel Song would be easier than some because of an underlying message. A wedding song, etc... would be other specific theme songs that would be somewhat similar.

Understand as the writer that the 'theme' type song is very specific. Every writer has a place... Every song has a place!! Inside that realm, it's very okay. Outside that realm, it is limited and therefore it's very DEAD!!

One great analogy is the category of Love Songs. They would be great for weddings! They would be perfect for a dance floor on slow songs. Again, every song has a place!

Non-Offensive

Although this is stronger for Gospel Music, it definitely applies to ANY type of music. Even rap has a particular audience and within that audience is people that WILL tolerate profanity and those that WILL NOT tolerate profanity.

Profanity is not the only thing that gets rather offensive. Even notations toward gender, race, etc... can be found extremely offensive.

I am an artist. I do like pushing the envelope a little because of the way I think. I don't like putting God in a little box and telling him what to do nor how to react. He made me just like he wanted me. However, the message you send within your songs sets a pattern that people will automatically judge and sum you up by... Hopefully, it would be one with respect.

Biblical Correctness

I know this sounds crazy to discuss about Country Music. But, this is true both with a Gospel Song or any other, including Country. It is more impactful for the Gospel Music song of course. For most types of songs OTHER than Gospel, it would be safer to say that whatever implications you may make, whether it be toward 'Heaven', or 'Our Creator', or possibly even something like 'the God above', make sure that it is within what 'most' people accept as being true.

An example of a Non-Gospel song making Biblical references is the ever popular 'God Bless The U.S.A.' by Lee Greenwood. He makes references to 'the God Above'. What would an Atheist think about the song?

Lee Greenwood knows that Country Music and Gospel Music are largely intertwined. Many Country Music artists actually cut a Gospel album, or project, every once in a while. Elvis Presley did. George Jones did.

Most Gospel Music songwriters and artists feel their music is a ministry. With that type of heart, everyone involved will feel it *A MUST* for your song to be Biblically Correct.

Even in other types of music, it is the exception that is more fun than the rule. I call it 'Writer's Prerogative'. You see, The Bible is very specific in some places and yet very vague in others. The writers paint a very vivid picture in some parables and tell only the highlights in others. There are many years that are seemingly missing in the lives of important people and yet just enough is given to get the point across. Noah, for example, is given a heritage in Genesis Chapter 5 and verses thereafter. However, not much is known or described about him except his connection with the Great Flood and lineages.

For instance… If I were to ask you what Noah's typical breakfast was or what kind of bed he slept on, you would have to rely on accepted norms from historians in reference to times. I just don't think that is specifically found in the Bible… But if I'm wrong, I would be open to your finding it.

Just as these writers only use the brush to stroke the painting right where they want you to see, you can do the same thing as a songwriter. I think a song that has sound doctrine and yet uses your imagination a bit in the construction leaves the listener to rely upon their own faith and belief to confirm the song's truth.

One example is the popular modern worship song 'I Can Only Imagine'. Even the very title suggests the song is crafted from the viewpoint and imagination of the author. He uses Biblical-Based Principles to back him up; but everything is accepted from the title and throughout the way to the end as if it is what the author and listeners might 'Imagine' it to be. Many times words like 'If', 'Hope', and 'Suppose' are used to create the same effect within lines of the song. With the use of those simple words, a theoretically unsound statement can be changed to be correct because the author only made the assumption that the statement 'may' be, or 'could be', correct.

There are tons of examples I could use. For the purpose of learning, I remember the old hymn 'No Tears In Heaven'. I also know that according to the Bible, God shall wipe away all our tears from our eyes.

Question…. Does that also mean that God cannot cry?

My main impression or thoughts about God and his ability to cry I found rested upon that old song. I had heard the song so much in growing up that I couldn't remember what the Bible actually said about it. That verse does not mean that there COULD NOT be tears in Heaven… No, it merely suggests that he will comfort us and there will be no need for crying. It does not say, nor suggest, that God did, could, or would never cry himself.

Having that idea in mind, I wrote a song called, "My SON" painting the picture of Crucifixion Day. The entire song, and my career it spurred along, is outlined in great detail in my book I have just suggested to you, 'The Long Road To NOWHERE'. The song came along when I was not using my gift of songwriting, or doing any writing for that matter. My entire writing career took an about face that particular morning. Get it and read about it!

In that book, there are neither fireworks nor vampire stories to keep your attention… No, there's just a story about a writer that wouldn't quit… but he didn't know why. He didn't, he wouldn't, and he couldn't. He was like everyone at times… on what seemed like a LONG ROAD that was leading him

NoWhere. I find it very comforting that God always knows right where we are… which tells me that we are definitely NOT NoWhere!! We're definitely somewhere; even if WE don't know where that is.

Again, the Gospel Music Song becomes somewhat of a ministry to the Gospel Music writer. To keep the listeners, the song MUST be Biblically Correct!

I have found though that a Great Writer can write wonderful songs no matter what the genre; and, most will want to try their wings. Writing a great song in Country Music is the same too!

Dance-Ability Factor

A great dancing song is a must!!

Whether it be the Honky Tonk or Love Song, everyone loves a great dance song with a great dance beat. From Line Dancing to Slow Dancing, people love to feel the music 'Come Alive' within them. There is probably no better genre of music to dance to than Country Music.

Country Music carries the understood perception of having a way of 'washing your troubles away'. A good Country Music slogan is 'If you've lost your lover - You can dance with another...'

Although I have just made that one up, it definitely fits in this genre of music. No matter what your troubles, the perception is that the music can make you feel good enough to eventually forget about them.

The cold truth is that it truly *will* be better for you in the long run than the alcohol consumption that typically goes along with it; especially in the Bars, Pubs, and Honky Tonks. At least you can *remember* what you're smiling about!

Catching Up

This segment consists of two parts: "Basic Facts of Writing Music" and "Forming a Song." I cover them more in-depth in my prior books but will touch on them here. It is a basic foundation in every song you will ever write. The genre doesn't matter. Mechanically, a song is a song like a car is a car. The ride only varies in the style, but either one will take you where you want to go. So, learn what makes up a song... and more importantly, learn WHY!!

Never overlook the basics. That's why I cover them here. It is not to assume you don't know anything about songwriting already because you probably do. It is like a football game. The team that has the best fundamentals will usually have the better chance to win. So, the more you practice and hear the basics, the better it comes to you without even thinking about it.

BASIC FACTS *of* WRITING MUSIC

In my book, 'How To Write Songs', I cover a more in-depth approach to the basics called 'BASIC FACTS of WRITING MUSIC'. Get it… study… study it again!!

How To Write Songs

Available on *KINDLE* and *NOOK*

There I discussed 8 elements that comprise most popular songs. Those are: The TITLE, The HOOK, The LYRIC, The MELODY, The STRUCTURE, The RANGE and KEY, The RHYTHM, and the HARMONY.

These are basic building blocks of a song that hold true in ANY song. The stronger those building blocks are, the stronger the song becomes. Therefore, the stronger the ability to write and understand these elements, the stronger the writer!

There are only 12 DIFFERENT musical notes available for us to use. That is all! I know that is hard to believe if you don't know much about music. This too is studied a bit more in-depth in my book, 'How To Write Songs', found on Kindle and Nook.

Every songwriter or composer that has ever lived took those same 12 notes and comprised entirely new songs. Is that not cool, or what?!! No one has more… No one has ever had less. Beethoven had… guess how many? You got it; only twelve different notes! Every other note is either an octave lower or higher; but is a duplicate… well, almost a duplicate!

An octave is technically, according to Wikipedia, *"is the interval between one musical pitch and another with half or double its frequency."* So, a note of 'A' above 'Middle C', at 440 Hz, would sound similar to our ears as the 'A' up the scale and double the frequency at 880 Hz. The next 'A' going downward on the scale, below 'Middle C', would be at half the frequency or at 220 Hz. Other than one seeming to be higher and the other one lower, our ears hear them as the same note.

Without trying to bore you, to finish up this idea Wikipedia says about an octave, *"notes an octave apart are given the same note name in the Western* *system of music notation—the name of a note an octave above A is also A. This is called **octave equivalency**, the assumption that pitches one or more octaves apart are musically equivalent"*.

Don't worry too much about memorizing all of this degree of technical stuff as a writer unless it peaks your interest. Just accept it and let's move on.

With this relatively small number of twelve unique notes, rhythmic patterns, and chord structures that are basic to most songs, believe it or not there are infinite numbers of possibilities in Songwriting.

So, here's one of my quick rules…

Study the SYSTEM…

Learn the SYSTEM…

Don't *Fight* the SYSTEM!!!

The best way to beat anything is to study it… track it… UNDERSTAND it!!

Here is where the more intense study helps in attempting to write a Hit Song in any genre. For us, it is trying to figure out what made it different from the others… that is the challenge. Many times there is NO DIFFERENCE!!

"What?" you might ask. The best way to explain it is that even with our best effort, we still cannot control the destiny of a song. The best shot we have is to write the very best song we can write; which after all was the writer's primary job in the first place! The rest of the formula will end up being determined by a host of people including singers, agents, producers, and ultimately, by the fans!

Understand the following basic concept well.

We have a tendency to write songs that sound very similar to today's hit songs. The reason is that the market responds to what most of the people want and demand in a certain genre. Because most of the people like a certain sound, they buy products in music that has that sound. Therefore, if they are buying 'THAT', the producers produce more of 'THAT'. If you listen to 'THAT', you tend to like 'THAT'… especially if you're buying 'THAT'. So, in this case, the 'THAT' means essentially that people like the songs that are selling and playing, or else they would buy different CD's and downloads. The market would then respond as the people demanded. Remember that SALES drives SUPPLY... even in the music business.

Let's say you tried to go out on a limb and create a very unique song... so unique in fact that it violated many rules. Do you think just two things could happen? Do you suppose that it might 1) go over very well... or 2) bomb out?

The truth is, it could do one of those two things... or it could very well fall almost anywhere in the middle between those extremes. It could go over well on a dance floor, but not do well on the radio. It could do well in bars and be despised in church. It could be listened to around school campuses and be banned by most parents. You see, a song takes its own path once it is created.

So we must understand and get a good grasp that how we craft a song may not necessarily guarantee people will love it, but it can almost guarantee people will hate it if it contains things people despise. Profanity and vulgarity will only be tolerated in a certain small segment of the market. And, even parents who love the bars actually prefer their young kids to NOT be exposed to that lifestyle. *UNDERSTAND THE RULES*!! There is a reason why it is suggested. *IT WORKS*!!

People tend to prefer faster songs over slower songs. Although I love both, I have come to realize the main difference is that people respond quickly to rhythm changes. A slow song usually has a 'deeper meaning' than the faster.

As a rule, faster songs generally make you happy and want to dance. Even if you don't dance visibly, you might be caught tapping your fingers on the desktop, window, or perhaps the steering wheel on the car. For whatever reason, something kicks in from deep within us when we hear certain rhythms and chords.

Duplicate a HIT-MAKER'S Habits!!

Remember to study, study, study and practice, practice, practice. That will mean you write, write, write.

If you will dwell on dissecting, studying, and implementing a Hit-Maker's Habits, you will soon be resonating some of the similar characteristics. At least then if your songs do not become hits, they still will be the best they can be. That is, after all, what we really wanted in the first place.

Forming A Song

Forming a song is easier than you think! It simply begins with an idea. It sounds hard but is really not. The best way to approach this, assuming you have no previous ideas is to brainstorm for a few topics or small phrases that peaks your interest. What you are looking for is something to build upon. There are no limits as long as the ideas and topics fall within the guidelines previously discussed.

From Love Songs to Gospel Songs and from Rock/Pop Songs to Country Music Songs, anything that comes to mind is probably okay. And, as you saw in the history of Country Music, the genre has evolved with sub-genres that the vast diversity is a huge plus for the writer.

Now that you have the topic or idea in place, you are ready to begin to structure the song. A strong musical background will help here. As a songwriter, I usually 'hear' a melody in my head as I construct the song. It keeps the syllables the right length on each line. Again, my book, 'How To Write Songs' on the Kindle or Nook, will strengthen these ideas on phrasing for you.

Generally speaking, if it is part of a STORY that is 'Taking You Somewhere', then you probably have come up with a line to fit into a verse. If it is pretty much the Object of the action (as if you are already there at that same somewhere), like the phrase 'My Home's In Alabama', then that is probably suited for the Chorus.

The reason being that in that case, you would use the chorus to tell the listener 'Why' and to set the stage for that particular line to be the center of attention. Then, you think of two or three 'Stories' or scenarios that can 'Stand Alone' telling an individual situation about your related subject. These situations would probably be the verses.

In verse one you could explain to the listener what is wrong. In verse two it would generally be another 'For Instance' citing to back up the story in the first verse.

In a case where you had several verses, the middle ones would either be a continuing story linking from one verse to the other, or they would be supporting verses citing more reasons… like the middle paragraphs of a letter.

Then in verse three, or the last one if there are many more, you would change directions and 'Head the Horses Home'… so to speak!! You hit your home-run with your audience and make the song apply to them directly and giving them advice on what to do to fix their problem.

This is the most important section of the song… this last verse coupled with the *last part of the chorus*. They give the plan of action, or focus of the entire song. Again, typically…

The Last Line of the Last Verse and

The Last Line of the Chorus

Gives the plan of action, or focus, of the ENTIRE SONG!!

You ALWAYS want to make sure that in writing Gospel or Christian Music, you give a 'Better Way', or SOLUTION, to their problem which should include God or some relevant idea (like Jesus, The Blood, Calvary, etc…). This can be done as boldly as the entire last verse or as subtly as the last line of the last verse. It could even possibly be done with just the right 'single word' or 'phrase', when placed at the right point… which is usually the last of the last verse. That points and pulls them right back into the Chorus, when sung the typical way.

Country Music tends to be more open. So, without the religious agenda, you have more options. It would be these same important lines, however, that 'sews up the basket!' Usually the hook is extremely catchy and found cleverly placed somewhere in these parts of the song.

More times than not, your idea or main phrase will end up at least mentioned in the Chorus… somewhere and somehow. It seems easier to construct a song from the Inside-Out or Backwards. It is sort of like hunting or fishing. How can that pertain to this, you ask?!

Most people go fishing to get to a certain particular spot where they intend to fish. They drive there *whichever* way gets them to that spot. They *park* at the nearest boat landing to where they intend to fish.

When they hunt, they know the particular field they will watch... *Where* they park and *how* they walk to that field is all determined AFTER they decide where their final destination will be.

Get this solidified in your head from an outline standpoint and it will all make a little more sense.

~~If you begin with a point that you put in the verse, you must try to figure out what you're trying to convey with that statement and THAT (what you're ultimately trying to convey) will end up being placed in, or as, your chorus. Likewise, if you put your idea in the Chorus, it is probably part of your MAIN idea and the OBJECT of the entire point or song. Therefore, you go back and come up with Supporting Ideas that 'back up' and lead them to... the chorus!!~~

If it is a 'story' type song, your verses may be either...

1 - Different individual stories each citing examples that lead you to the Chorus.

2 - A continuation type story where one verse continues the same story where the other one quit.

With all of that in mind, let me mention the basic building block of a song!

Building A Chorus

I have already covered this section better in my previous book, 'How To Write Songs - How To Write a HIT SONG'. It is available on both Kindle and Nook.

The main points I want to make should be reviewed here too.

1 -   Decide On A Topic

2 -   Who What Where How

3 -   Narrow Down the Point Of View

4 -   Decide - ONE-Sentence Phrase

5 -   Decide - Where it may Fit

6 -   Decide - Object or Beginning

7 -   If Object then it is probably the Last Line

8 -   Profound Statement

9 -   Second Line Supports

10 -   Bridge The Gap

Decide On A Topic - This can be the hardest or easiest of all the work. Sometimes as writers we all draw blanks. Perhaps it is not a 'Writing Day' as I like to refer to some. For some, it is easier to build something once we can get jump started. For others, the ideas come easily and it is the craft that seems hard. Here, we are helping you with both.

Who What Where How - Ask yourself... Who, What, Where, How... This is just a brainstorming technique whereby when you answer some basic questions you will give your song an outline or perimeter in which to work.

Narrow Down the Point Of View - Narrow down the point of view about the topic. If you thought about something specific, you may be ready now.

Decide - ONE-Sentence Phrase - Make a decision about a ONE Sentence phrase, or at least a few words phrase, that makes the point the best.

Decide - Where it may Fit - Decisions, decisions... you will think. If you have really done your work right and come up with this precise phrase, then deciding where it may fit will not be so hard.

Decide - Object or Beginning - Generally speaking, if it is part of a story that is 'Taking You Somewhere', then you probably have come up with a line to fit into a verse. If it is pretty much the Object of the action (as if you are already there), like the phrase 'Everything is better in Dixie', then that is probably suited for the Chorus.

If Object then it is probably the Last Line - If it is the Object, then it is probably best fitted as the last sentence of the Chorus.

Profound Statement - Come up with a profound statement that *begins* or *initiates* this action, command, or statement. If your object phrase was placed as your last line, say line four, then here you make a profound statement to begin the chorus.

Second Line Supports - The second line either supports the first line as a stand-alone sentence or can be a run-on with the first line. As a general rule it SHOULD rhyme with the ending word on line four provided that is the particular scheme you may use.

Bridge The Gap - Line number three bridges the gap between the other lines and makes it all make sense. *If it is too much to be said in four lines and the writer simply needs more lines*, then look at it as an eight line chorus with lines two and four rhyming and six and eight rhyming.

NOTE*   The Chorus and Verses do NOT have to rhyme alike. Some will and some won't. This statement refers to the Chorus vs. Verse. Each Verse DOES need to rhyme similarly to each other. More about rhyming can be found in my book, 'How To Write Songs' on the Kindle or Nook.

Important Points
~This -*n*- That~

~The best way to see what people are looking for and will be willing to jump on and purchase is by studying the charts and *examining the current Chart-Topping titles*. That gives you a better understanding of what is Commercial.

~The TITLE may very well be the VERY LAST THING about the song that you write!! You may have the song completely finished and it still have no title! That is definitely okay! You will learn as you begin to study the craft, that few writers know the title to their songs in the early stages of writing any particular song. Don't worry because with a little practice, you will see that you will know the song inside-out. That means that just by glancing at your word repetitions and placements, you can get a 'feel' for a good title.

~*Use Innovative Ideas* for the lyric. Think of something new, a different angle about something already said, or an old subject that is said in a new way. Also avoid making it too personal whereby you exclude some. Call things like 'cancer' or 'leukemia' by a different name trying to be inclusive… like perhaps 'sickness' or 'disease'. That way, it probably has happened to most everyone at some time or another and isn't so specific.

~Excessive words should be avoided. Say what you need in as few words as possible. You might need a 'filler' word due to the syllables, but no one should have 'filler phrases'. Make every phrase important.

~The melody of a song should be catchy and easy to sing.

~Change the Rhythm, Change the Song!!

Should I say this again? …Can't decide how a song should be sung? Try different things…

…again… *Change the Rhythm, Change the Song*!!

~The Simple Songs are the most memorable!

~Keep it in a reasonable range of notes. As a rule…

If *YOU* can't sing it, *don't write it*!!

WRITING THE SONG

Putting It All Together

Okay, so now you're excited. You have read some rules carefully and you're ready to begin writing. We now will study the Hit Song!

RELAX!! Let's do it!!

I must offer a few basic assumptions for this hand-on actual writing exercise that culminates all of the things we have learned. The reason is that since I am writing this and not talking to you in person, I cannot ask you questions.

You cannot hear any music when reading a book. So, we will eliminate the element of music and concentrate on lyrics.

Please note this will work for any genre of music.

I am not the writer of most of the songs used. They will be very big 'Hit Songs' from Country Music. I'll take a fun approach to dissecting them.

So, now with the idea that a song should follow a template, see one below:

TITLE

V1 - X - X - X - X
X - X - X - X
X - X - X - X
X - X - X - X

CHORUS X - X - X - X
X - X - X - X
X - X - X - X
X - X - X - X

V2 - X - X - X - X
X - X - X - X
X - X - X - X
X - X - X - X

This template is just a generic one. And, trust me when I say that many songs vary from a canned template. It is easier for the human mind to 'see' things when placed into some kind of a template; even if it breaks some rules.

An example… A poem with five lines and an odd rhyming scheme would still be easier to establish verse to verse when placed on paper and in some format. As long as the same places in each verse match the odd rhyming scheme, it just might work.

Hit Songs are not Hit Songs because they are different; although many times they are… They are Hit Songs because they are GREAT SONGS and they WORK!! Remember, you can violate the rules if you understand them!! The more you sing/work on your craft, the easier your Gift tells you what works!!

A Song or THREE
(Hands-On-Practice)

Song Number One ~~

Let's take this first one straight on. We will look at it without hesitation where you know exactly what the song is when you're looking at the lyrics.

According to Wikipedia...

""**I'm So Lonesome I Could Cry**" is a song written and recorded by American country music singer-songwriter Hank Williams in 1949. The song about loneliness was largely inspired by his troubled relationship with wife Audrey Sheppard. With evocative lyrics, such as the opening lines "Hear that lonesome whip-poor-will/He sounds too blue to fly," the song has been covered by a wide range of musicians."

"I'm So Lonesome I Could Cry"

Hear that lonesome whippoorwill
He sounds too blue to fly
The midnight train is whining low
I'm so lonesome I could cry

I've never seen a night so long
When time goes crawling by
The moon just went behind the clouds
To hide its face and cry

Did you ever see a robin weep
When leaves begin to die?
Like me, he's lost the will to live
I'm so lonesome I could cry

The silence of a falling star
Lights up a purple sky
And as I wonder where you are
I'm so lonesome I could cry

We begin our analysis noting that Hank Williams, the writer, had a troubled relationship that the encyclopedia says was a primary contributor to the sentiments of this song. That is about as official as you can get unless you knew Hank Williams personally and could dispute it.

We covered a section called 'Major Components or Factors of the Country Music Song'. Number five was 'Touch Everyone's Emotions'. This song is a picture-perfect example of that.

Hank Williams was hurting. And, his audiences knew it. Many of them were hurting inside too from different relationships and situations. As a matter of fact, I dare say there isn't a person alive who has had some hardship at least at some time or another. Therefore, EVERYONE can identify with the song. They can 'feel' the pain and the 'lonely' feeling he is experiencing.

People have an inherent need to 'identify' with things. For some reason, they want to 'talk' to someone about it. In this case, the song 'does the talking' for them. It also, unfortunately, aided the notion that 'drunks' liked to 'drown in their sorrows'. Whether you like it or not, it became extremely popular.

How did he do it?

It was simple. The song doesn't have to be fancy... It just has to be good!! It has to be 'sing-able' and it has to be 'memorable'. Good songs are all of that and more!

He began by citing one of the most lonesome sounds anyone might hear. I don't really know the range of the whippoorwill. It may be just a southern bird. But, coming from the south, I have heard it many times. When you are alone in the quiet countryside at night, it is a 'Southern Living' paradigm and example at its very finest. The sound will be found to echo across many a lonesome valley or country road on a still, quiet night.

Hank follows most of the typical rules of writing.

He rhymes lines 2 with 4. Each of the 4 verses has the same number of syllables and phrasing and it is easy to sing.

One of his variations is that it has No Chorus. That is not the 'norm', but it is acceptable. The old hymns, 'Just As I Am' and 'Amazing Grace', likewise does not have a Chorus. So, it can be done.

He makes a 2nd reference to a lonesome sound… the Midnight Train Whistle. This too would echo across hills and valleys if you lived near the railroad tracks, within a mile or so of a crossing, and the train had a scheduled trip at night.

His 2nd verse makes reference to the moon also 'hiding' its face. He gives it the personification of doing just what people do in shame and loneliness. Naturally, we know the moon doesn't respond to our individual feelings. But, it works well in this song to exemplify someone's dejected feelings.

In verse 3, Hank makes a reference to himself. Here's where he uses the song to place a personal implication. He also uses the Robin, something everyone full well knows might prefer the spring time, to visualize its probable spurn or disdain of the coming wintertime.

And then, in verse 4, Hank drives the point home making it personable to both the listener and the other party in his relationship. He states…

*'And as I wonder where you are
I'm so lonesome I could cry'.*

That gave a profound statement and leaving the word 'you' as to mean whomever it might pertain. If he had named a name, it could be too personal. But this way, everyone or anyone could be the 'you'.

This song is not a 'continuation' story song but one where the paragraphs 'support' the idea; like the body of a letter. Then, the last one drives the point home making it apply personally to the listener and writer alike.

…Great Song!!

Song Number TWO ~~

We'll do this one a little differently. We'll look at it blind at first.

This highlighted Country Music song is a 'love song' of sorts. It doesn't have the typical 'love song' slow beat that people want to slow-dance to though.

Here we think of how the many ways we experience love and the way it makes us feel. We think of how a song might characterize the wedding ring and its traditional symbolic meaning being endless and never-ending from the implications of it being round.

This song carries it one step further and outlines the feelings and desires that one feels when in love. However, this particular song comes from the angle of 'falling' in love instead of 'being' in love.

Even more than that, it talks of the 'desires' that you feel when in love. It tells of how deep the desires are… but never describes anything that could taken the wrong way by anyone in any culture. The conservative *Bible Belt* areas even embraced the song even more than most of the others.

It is a simple song with a ton of 'fiery' thoughts…

What song am I talking about?

I'll still let you guess.

It talks about love being a 'burning' thing'. Later, the song says… 'The taste of love is sweet… When hearts like ours meet.'

Now do you know what song I am talking about? Well, here it is!!

The Ring of Fire

<u>Verse 1</u>

Love   is a burning' thing,

And it makes   a fiery ring

Bound   by wild desire

I fell into   a ring of fire.

<u>CHorus</u>

I fell into

a burnin' ring of fire

I went down, down, down

And the flames went higher,

And it burns, burns, burns

The ring of fire

the ring of fire.

<u>Verse 2</u>

The taste   of love is sweet

When hearts   like ours meet

I fell for you   like a child

Oh, but   the fire ran wild.

In verse one, it simply makes a statement...

'Love   is a burning' thing,'

This simple statement begins the song like a letter. This opening statement is carried on in line 2...

'And it makes   a fiery ring'

I believe the writers wanted to end the phraseology of Verse One with the title; or it seems to feel that way. So, at that point, here's what you have...

Love   is a burning' thing,
And it makes   a fiery ring
X X X X X X X X
X X X X   a ring of fire

It is my opinion that after the stated fact in the first two lines, line 3 actually begins a new statement and it ends up being the last two lines put together.

Bound   by wild desire
I fell into   a ring of fire

The rhyming scheme for the verses is A-B and so lines 1 and 2 rhyme and then 3 and 4 rhyme. Notice the 2nd verse does actually mimic the rhyming pattern to verse one. This is a good thing.

The chorus actually strays a bit! Sometimes the writer can't pull it off when it is this far off-balance. There are actually 7 lines, not 8, in the chorus. When I go back and sing it to myself, it feels as if it is a 4/4 song Time Signature with probably a 2/4 measure at the end of the chorus.

Lines 2 and 4 rhyme with 'fire' and 'higher'. But then, they go and do a repeat pattern of line 3 (with 'Down, Down, Down') and match with (it 'burns, burns, burns').

I think that is why they kept the next two lines with both the Title phrase and the rhyme; therefore also keeping it rhyming with 'fire' and 'higher'. So, to everyone's ear, it sounds like it really does rhyme well; even though it doesn't have the usual evenly-matched number of syllables. It is almost like your ear is 'forgiving' to it because of the fondness everyone has with the nice patterns of 'down,down,down' and 'burns, burns, burns'.

Verse 2 rhymes well just like Verse 1. This makes it the song stronger, usually. They begin the verse with another simple statement...

The taste   of love is sweet
When hearts   like ours meet

The well-embellished words like 'taste of love' make this a wonderful line. Any and every one who has ever known or experienced love can identify with this. I don't know what people may picture the 'taste of love' actually tasting like... but one doesn't have to know. The picture is painted so beautifully with the words.

I fell for you   like a child
Oh, but   the fire ran wild

And then, in the last two lines, they make it personal and hit the home run! Everyone knows how a wildfire can spread and how fast it can run. It almost seems to be 'running' if the underbrush is extremely dry! Great song again!

According to <u>Wikipedia</u>...

""**Ring of Fire**" or "**The Ring of Fire**" is a country music song popularized by Johnny Cash and co-written by June Carter Cash (wife of Johnny Cash) and Merle Kilgore. The single appears on Cash's 1963 compilation album, *Ring of Fire: The Best of Johnny Cash*. The song was originally recorded by June's sister, Anita Carter, on her Mercury Records album *Folk Songs Old and New* (1963) as "(Love's) Ring of Fire".

The song was recorded on March 25, 1963, and became the biggest hit of Johnny Cash's career, staying at number one on the charts for seven weeks. It was certified Gold on 1/21/2010 by the R.I.A.A."

Awesome Life-Changing Story

Before I can highlight the next song, I must tell a quick story. If you think I'm wasting your time, please reconsider. It has been said that writing is fifty percent perspiration and fifty percent inspiration. The perspiration will change the outcome; but it is the inspiration that will change your life!!

With that being true, you will begin to take notice of the little things that will inspire you to write. It is those small lessons that fuel the determination in our own writing. And, perhaps it is the impatience that stops us all from appreciating the little things that we see later in life that molded our paths in the first place.

"Are the little things that important?" you ask.

Picture one-fourth of a sandwich... a simple quarter of a sandwich. Chances are, it wouldn't probably 'light your fire'. But, if you hadn't eaten in two days, that same simple three inch by three inch piece of bread and meat becomes a gourmet lunch!

Writers wait and wait for an opportunity... any opportunity. Once it arrives, you will find that there were small, very small pivoting points in your life that were really giant pivoting boulders that took you there. That's right... the little things are vastly important. Now, for the story...

Jerry and Johnny

They were just two young, local boys that had a great talent. They could play the guitar and sing. The first one, Gerald House, had a great sense of humor which led to him being quick on his feet when he was onstage.

The second was also very talented and, as it has turned out through the years, is a very close friend of mine, Johnny Duren.

The setting was the small town of Gordo, Alabama. The time, well, it was many, many years ago. I wasn't even born yet. Gasoline was very cheap; and yet, very expensive because wages weren't much at all.

Here's the story...

Johnny writes about himself, "Gerald "Jerry" House and Johnny Duren of Gordo, AL started singing together when they were freshmen in high school. They sang at different school events for a year or so then formed a country music band and entered a talent contest that was produced by the Grand Ole' Opry and the Pet Milk Company. At age 16 they entered the local version of the contest that was held in Columbus, MS and promoted by radio station WCBI. Radio stations all across the nation held local contests and chose winners to be judged by someone on the national level.

Jerry and Johnny won the local contest in Columbus, then went to the radio station and recorded a tape of a couple of songs to be sent to Nashville to be considered for national honors. They were chosen as one of six finalists to compete in Nashville. This was years ago and communication was not what it is today. In fact neither of their families even had telephones. However one of the guys in the band had a phone and he was the contact person for the band.

Pet Milk and Grand Ole' Opry only wanted the two singers to come to Nashville for the contest, but Jerry and Johnny said they would not go unless the entire band could go. So, they invited the entire group to come to Nashville with all expenses paid.

Some of the other names who were finalists included Melba Montgomery who recorded many albums with George Jones, Johnny Tillotson who had several country hits, and the winner was Margie Bowes. Margie later married Doyle Wilburn of the Wilburn Brothers. She became a member of the Grand Ole' Opry. Margie was from North Carolina, Melba was from Florence, AL, Johnny Tillotson was from Florida. There was one contestant from West Virginia and one from Texas.

Jerry and Johnny sang together for about 15 years. Jerry moved to Nashville and started writing songs. Johnny started singing in a Gospel Quartet and began writing songs as well.

Jerry has received BMI awards for his songwriting, having written songs that were recorded by such artists as George Morgan, Kitty Wells, Connie Smith and Mel Tillis. Johnny has had several gospel songs recorded by local groups and is still singing with his friend Joe Brown. They call themselves "*The Songs of Faith*" and can be contacted on Facebook."

As Johnny Duren is telling me this story, he fills me in on another tidbit of very intriguing personal information. I was elated and blown away!

Johnny goes on, "It so happened to be that, in the middle of that story about the 'going to Nashville part', Gerald (Jerry) House sent word back that there was no way without the band... It was the entire group or nothing. What he didn't tell them was that there was no way the fathers and mothers was going to let the boys go that far by themselves and without any money, a suitable vehicle, etc...

One of the band members needed a guitar amp. He didn't know where he could get one. So, they made a detour on the way to Nashville by way of my dad's house in the extremely small Western Alabama town of Belk, Alabama.

When Johnny told the story, he said...

"Your dad, knowing Hayes Skelton one of our band members, was willing to let him borrow the amp because he had done some guitar playing with your dad, Mr. Calvin Jones and his sisters, Martha and Frances, your aunts. Anyway, your dad came out of the house with the amp. But before he would let us leave, he had us roll down the car window and then he stuck his head inside."

Johnny continued, "Mark, your dad looked the teenagers over and said, "Boys, now I am letting Hayes borrow the amp. Don't you get the notion that anyone else can just come when you want to and borrow my amp… BECAUSE YOU _CAN'T_ AND YOU _AIN'T_!!"""

Johnny and I both laughed. I had not heard this story before. I realized that although my dad was a hard man to get to know, he really would have helped them in any way he could. The difference was, times were hard and he was used to people NOT bringing things back in the condition they borrowed them in. Sometimes, they wouldn't bring them back at all. Although my dad has passed away now, through the years I can just hear my dad saying, "And son, any way you look at it, that is just called _STEALING_!!"

As much as I hated to admit his sarcasm, he was right! Who would have ever guessed that a seemingly insignificant guitar amplifier would have at least played a part in the 'history' of the making of the song that I am about to highlight.

Song Number THREE ~~

This highlighted Country Music song is very special to me because of the story I have just told. For you see, it is here that we pick back up with the story.

None other than the same Gerald (Jerry) House ends up a few years later while in front of a well-known singer in Nashville at something called a 'Guitar Pulling'. That is where songwriters sit around and take turns pitching songs to an artist who is ready to cut an album (in those days and now it is called a project).

Many times, back then, the artist would learn the song on the spot as he cut it in the studio. It wasn't necessarily practiced for weeks or months before recording.

It was one of those kinds of 'Guitar Pulling' days. The artist was Mel Tillis, the now very popular Country Music singer and songwriter.

According to Johnny Duren, his friend Jerry House was asked to do his... which he did play his guitar and sing his songs to pitch to Mel. At the end of the allotted time, Mel asked them, "Is that 'all you got'?"

Each writer looked at the others and no one was prepared for an entire rejection session.

Finally, Jerry looked up and said, "Well, there is one more I could do. But, it's kind of crazy..."

"Let's hear it!" Mel blurted.

Jerry began to play and sing the song. I don't think Mel even let him get to the end.

Mel jumped up on the small end table there in the center of the room and shouted, "IT'S A HIT, IT'S A HIT!!"

Mel called another Country Music star of the 1960's named Del Reeves. Del later became a music executive having a large part in signing Billy Ray Cyrus.

Back to the story, Mel Tillis called Del Reeves and told him about the song, "I got The Hoss". His reasoning was that Mel really thought it would be even better suited for Del.

Just as things sometimes take unlikely turns, Del's response was, "Well if it is so good, then why aren't you doing it?"

Mel thought a minute and said, "Okay, I'll just do that!!" once he realized that Del wasn't as interested as probably Mel thought he should have been.

They began right that moment working with Mel's band and recording it. The problem was, there was only about four hours allotted for that session.

That song took about three of the hours. As the time dragged on, the writers got disgusted and left the building. When the song was finished and they were ready for the other songs, most of the writers had left. So, Mel actually took a few more of Jerry House's songs to fill the album just from being in the right place at the right time… and waiting patiently. The other writers' impatience and leaving the session had cost them their cuts.

Now, here's the song….

I Got The Hoss

<u>Verse 1</u>

Hey baby, let me see your brand new saddle
Let's that pretty thing up on my horse
Let's get it on real tight now
'Cause we don't want you falling off

<u>CHorus</u>

Well, I got the horse and you got the saddle
We like to ride side by side
Aw, I got the horse and she got the saddle
Together we're gonna ride, ride, ride

<u>Verse 2</u>

In the moonlight by the river
By the honeysuckle vine
We'll be riding, peeping and hiding
Till we see the morning light

<u>CHorus</u>

Well, I got the horse and you got the saddle
We like to ride side by side
Aw, I got the horse and she got the saddle
Together we're gonna ride, ride, ride

<u>Verse 3</u>

Hey, baby, let's stop for a little while
I need to give my old horse a rest
And you know there ain't no use
In us trying to wear out your new saddle

<u>Verse 4</u>

Hear the crickets singing softly
Never heard a sweeter sound
And you know crickets do their singing

By just rubbing their legs around

CHorus
Well, I got the horse and you got the saddle
We like to ride side by side
Aw, I got the horse and she got the saddle
Together we're gonna ride, ride, ride

CHorus
Well, I got the horse and you got the saddle
We like to ride side by side
Aw, I got the horse and she got the saddle
Together we're gonna ride, ride, ride

First of all, in dissecting this song, we notice that Johnny was right... it is a 'Crazy' song. It has tons of 'implications'. Most are somewhat targeting lovers. Notice he never crossed the line. If he had, a conservative audience as was the Grand Ole' Opry would not have stayed with him. They could, however, appreciate the implications recognizing the human side of us all.

It appears to have 4 Verses with the chorus repeated many times. This arrangement is very effective but only if you can keep the audience's attention.

Mel Tillis, as was wildly known, had a speech impediment. In other words, he stuttered. Apparently, if he could 'sing' the words, he did well. The stuttering came when he tried to talk.

The music for the song had a simple chord structure using the 1,4,5 chords of the scale. With the moving beat, Mel figured out that he could 'talk' on the appropriate verses and actually stutter on purpose. He made sure it was the last word, usually 'saddle'. To do this, he would pause for several seconds right before the word so that every person in the audience, both in person and on TV, was sitting on the edge of his/her seat; and without even knowing it, they seemed to involuntarily try to 'help' Mel anticipate getting the word to come out.

This gimmick worked. If it were not a gimmick, Mel would have only done 'singing' songs. No, this went over perfect. Right after the last word was 'sputtered', he would be ready to tear off with the next verse.

As far as structure, this song isn't perfect. There aren't tons of true rhymes. The structure is definitely has the Chorus rhyming on lines 2 and 4 with 'side' and 'ride'. It seems to be calling for the verses to rhyme lines 2 and 4 as well. Let's take a look at those in particular.

Verse one has 'horse' and 'off'. These are not quite even similar except for the 'O' used as the vowel.

Verse two has 'vine' and 'light'. Again, these are not quite so similar. They do have the same vowels, though, which is the 'I'.

Verse three is not even an attempted rhyme. "Why would Jerry do this?"

The answer is, I don't know. I will say that when I looked at this long and hard, it hit me that this was one of the recitation verses. So, the rhyming scheme got lost in the shuffle to the listener's ear as they heard him hesitate in speaking the last word 'Saddle'.

Then, immediately, he sang Verse four which actually has a perfect rhyme with 'sound' and 'around'. The audience is clapping wildly, by that time in the song, and 'eating out of his hand', so to speak.

If a song can do that and take the country by storm, nothing else matters. Done any other way, the song probably would not have made it. I think Jerry House knew it. That is why he didn't pitch it as his first pitch at the 'Guitar Pulling'.

As a writer, don't underestimate your songs. Just try to match a song with the right artist when pitching. Then, write, write, write and pitch, pitch, pitch!! Who knows… one day your dad's guitar amp might just make a little change in the history of something as huge as Country Music!!

Song Number FOUR ~~

This highlighted Country Music song is, too, a 'love song' of sorts. Fittingly and purposefully selected, it was written by none other than the famous Country Music writer, Mel Tillis.

This song shows how controversial a song can be and how it can very well either help you or hurt you. Kenny Rogers was not the first one to record it; nor was he the last. It was also recorded by Waylon Jennings and Roger Miller. But, it became the biggest hit for Kenny Rogers.

The song has obvious underlying controversial meanings. Without any other information, it seems like a song you would shy away from as an artist. However, artists like 'different' kinds of songs. They like to 'make a name' for themselves and so they sometimes seek and are attracted to this type of controversial music. Although it paid off for Kenny Rogers, it could have, and almost did, backfire just as easily.

People have a tendency to 'like what they like'!! As I mentioned earlier, people have different desires and tastes whether we, as writers, like it or not. It is so imperative for us to recognize these 'cravings', if you will, and capitalize off them. We MUST be careful not to allow it to backlash on us!

As an example, people actually 'crave' different things... like chocolate. Someone who loves chocolate was pretty much born that way. To others who don't, they don't have any innate cravings that they must fight. But to the Choc-o-holics, it becomes a never-ending battle inside themselves.

The battle is not so much to entirely stay away from it; but mostly to 'eat just a little'. It is the stopping that is hard for them. Like a powerful drug, it can make them overeat, and ultimately drive their blood sugar to dangerous levels.

We all recognize that, although we shouldn't tell someone else how to live or what to do, people should only eat in moderation. It is common sense that it just can't be good for you to go to extremes with this.

Well, to the people who like 'different' kinds of songs, it is equally as hard to explain. Sometimes people end up liking or loving a song that they actually despise the internal message of. Perhaps that is because they love a Hook Line; perhaps it is a certain Musical Phrase; or perhaps they even just 'love' the singer.

Many of The BEATLES' songs were so zany that I dare say almost half the people did not know the real meanings of the songs. They loved the sound and musical phrases and so they just sang along and appreciated the song for its musical work and not necessarily the meaning.

In a controversial song, coupled with today's media, this is tremendously more important than ever. People will exploit and highlight anything they wish to disagree with; and if they detest it, they will push the negative to the brink.

Let's look at the song… and then you will see the story behind the song and understand how it could have been disaster.

Ruby Don't Take Your Love To Town

You've painted up your lips and rolled and curled your tinted hair
Ruby are you contemplating going out somewhere
The shadows on the wall tell me the sun is going down
Oh Ruby, don't take your love to town

For it wasn't me that started that old crazy Asian war
But I was proud to go and do my patriotic chores
And I know Ruby that I'm not the man I used to be
But Ruby, I still need your company

It's hard to love a man whose legs are bent and paralyzed
And the wants and the needs of a woman your age, Ruby I realize
But it won't be long I've heard them say until I'm not around
Oh Ruby, don't take your love to town

She's leavin' now for I just heard the slamming of the door
The way I know I've heard it slam a hundred times before
If I could move I'd get my gun and put her in the ground
Oh Ruby, don't take your love to town

Don't take your love to town for my sake turn around

This song is about a woman named 'Ruby'. It doesn't say she is the man's wife; but it would be presumed so. It seems to be of a person injured and crippled. It speaks of 'old crazy Asian War', but doesn't definitively say that is how he was injured. It also has suggestive themes and hints to his inadequacy to do what lovers do because of bent legs and knees. It also addresses *'And the wants and the needs of a woman your age'* with this statement somewhat as well.

So, obviously she puts on makeup and leaves him going into town to probably 'be with' someone else. He begs her not to go... but she goes.

He then eludes to *'If I could move I get my gun and put her in the ground'*. Obviously, he is wanting to 'end' this problem for him.

As far as the song itself, it rhymes well. It has an A-B, A-B pattern with line 1 rhyming with line 2; and then line 3 with line 4.

Also notice, it has FOUR VERSES and NO CHORUS!! This is unique for sure!

Behind The Song -

This forthcoming explanation is taken from www.SongFacts.com

"Mel Tillis wrote this. He based the song on a couple who lived near his family in Florida. In real life, the man was wounded in Germany in World War II and sent to recuperate in England. There he married a nurse who took care of him at the hospital. The two of them moved to Florida shortly afterward, but he had periodic return trips to the hospital as problems with his wounds kept flaring up. His wife saw another man as the veteran lay in the hospital.

Tillis changed the war in the song to the Korean War, and left out the life ending: the man killed her in a murder-suicide. In the song, the man says he would killer if he could move to get his gun.

This was originally recorded by Johnny Darrell, whose version was a Country hit in 1967. Rogers had the biggest hit with the song, but it was also recorded by Waylon Jennings and Roger Miller.

A lot of controversy surrounded this song when it became a hit for Kenny Rogers in 1969, as the Vietnam War was raging and the song was often assumed to be about a man who came home crippled from that war. Rogers would perform the song in a jovial manner, and the crowd would often clap and sing along, so to some it was seen as disrespectful to veterans.

In a 1970 interview with *Beat Instrumental*, Rogers defended the song, saying: "Look, we don't see ourselves as politicians, even if a lot of pop groups think they are in the running for a Presidential nomination. We are there, primarily, to entertain. Now if we can entertain by providing thought-provoking songs, then that's all to the good. But the guys who said 'Ruby' was about Vietnam were way off target – it was about Korea. But whatever the message, and however you interpret it, fact is that we wouldn't have looked at it if it hadn't been a GOOD song. Just wanna make good records, that's all.""

According to Wikipedia...

""**Ruby, Don't Take Your Love to Town**" is a song written by Mel Tillis. The song was made famous by Kenny Rogers and the First Edition in 1969. "Ruby" was originally recorded in 1967 by Johnny Darrell, who scored a number nine country hit with it that year.

In 1969, after Kenny Rogers and the First Edition's success with the hits "Just Dropped In (To See What Condition My Condition Was In)" and "But You Know I Love You", Rogers wanted to take his group more into a country music direction. They recorded their version of the song (with Rogers singing the lead) in one take. The record was a major hit for them. It made #1 in the UK on the *New Musical Express* (#2 on the BBC chart) staying in the top twenty for 15 weeks and selling over a million copies by the end of 1970. In the United States it reached number six on the Hot 100 and number thirty-nine on the country chart and also sold more than 1 million copies by 1979. Worldwide, the single sold more than 7 million copies.

In 1977, now a solo act following the First Edition's split in early-1976, Rogers made re-recordings of this and a number of other First Edition hits for his 1977 greatest hits package *Ten Years Of Gold* (later issued in the British Isles as *The Kenny Rogers Singles Album*), which topped the US country charts and was just as successful in the United Kingdom."

Song Number FIVE ~~

Song Number Five is a crazy and almost whacky song. It is the type of song that you probably wouldn't like at the first pass because of the 'Childish' and 'Whacky' hook line… Achy-Breaky-Heart.

By now, I'm quite sure you've probably heard it no matter what type of music you prefer. And, it probably has gotten on your nerves. Without a doubt, it falls into the category of being one of the songs that I was talking about earlier. You know, the one where you are addicted but can't help it despite your intentions. Yes, the Choc-o-Holic comparison.

The first time I heard it, I thought it was just too 'crazy' or 'zany' to be a hit. After listening, I found myself almost wanting to dance to it every time it came on the radio. I suspect I wasn't the only person in the world who did also.

So, what is it about a song like this that simply works? What is it that takes over in your body and wants to dance despite your fighting it?

Answer that question and you will have just learned how to predict hits before they happen. You'll find that whatever works, you should learn to duplicate it in your songs! So, let's examine it.

TWO CHORDS!!... that's all it has is TWO CHORDS!! The one (home) chord, which I believe is 'A' and then the five chord, which I think is 'E'. So as you see, a song doesn't have to necessarily be complicated to be a hit… it just has to be a GOOD SONG!!

Don puts an internal rhyme in Line 1 and then another mirroring in Line 3. This technique is VERY effective!! The rhyming scheme is A-B, C-B. In other words, lines 2 and 4 are the rhyming lines outside the internal rhymes. This pattern holds true in the chorus as well.

Also note, that the internal rhymes in lines 1 and 3 in the chorus are the same actual words 'Heart'.

It is hard to say that any Hit Song has a weakness. But if I were to be pressed to find one, my opinion would put it the LAST LINE of the Chorus and possibly even the entire Verse 3. Personally, I would have changed all of that. If the writer has personal ties to the story line though, he will fight the artist to leave it alone. And thus, sometimes a song is released anyway.

Achy Breaky Heart lyrics
Songwriter: Don Von Tress

<u>Verse 1</u>
You can tell the world you never was my girl
You can burn my clothes when I'm gone
Or you can tell your friends just what a fool I've been
And laugh and joke about me on the phone

<u>Verse 2</u>
You can tell my arms, go back onto the phone
You can tell my feet to hit the floor
Or you can tell my lips to tell my fingertips
They won't be reaching out for you no more

<u>CHorus</u>
But don't tell my heart, my achy breaky heart
I just don't think it'd understand
And if you tell my heart, my achy breaky heart
He might blow up and kill this man

<u>Verse 3</u>
You can tell your Ma I moved to Arkansas
You can tell your dog to bite my leg
Or tell your brother Cliff who's fist can tell my lips
He never really liked me anyway

<u>Verse 4</u>
Oh tell your aunt Louise, tell anything you please
Myself already knows that I'm not okay
Oh you can tell my eyes to watch out for my mind
It might be walking out on me today

"Written by the Country songwriter and performer Don Von Tress, this was a remake of a 1991 song by the Country act The Marcy Brothers, titled "Don't Tell My Heart." That original version had the lyrics: "Don't tell my heart, my achy, breakin' heart...""

According to <u>Wikipedia</u>...

"Achy Breaky Heart" is a hit country music song written by Don Von Tress. Originally titled "Don't Tell My Heart" and recorded by The Marcy Brothers in 1991, its name was later changed to "Achy Breaky Heart" and recorded by Billy Ray Cyrus on his 1992 album *Some Gave All*. As Cyrus' debut single and signature song, it made him famous and has been his most successful song. It became the first single ever to achieve triple Platinum status in Australia and the 1992's best selling single in the same country.

In the United States became a crossover hit on pop and country radio, peaking at number 4 on the Billboard Hot 100 and topping the Hot Country Singles & Tracks chart, becoming the first Country single to be certified Platinum since Kenny Rogers and Dolly Parton's "Islands in the Stream" in 1983. The single topped in several countries and after being featured on *Top of the Pops*, peaked at number 3 on the UK Singles Chart. It remains Cyrus's biggest hit single in the USA to date, and his only one to reach the Top 10 of the Billboard Hot 100. Thanks to the video of this hit, there was the explosion of the *line-dance* into the mainstream, becoming a craze.

Summary

Many great potential songwriters have never picked up a pen because they were stopped before they ever started. Yes, it's true. Many wonderful songs were impeded by the writer themselves because they failed; not because they failed at songwriting, but rather because they failed to act at all.

Learning the craft of songwriting involves a great deal in the participation of the study and practice of the art.

So I ask you, "How Can a Writer Write?" It's truly hard to say. I would be the first to begin to talk about things like 'Gifts', 'Something we're Good at', 'it's our Thing', etc…

Personally, I believe that God gave us those 'Gifts' and certain opportunities that will come our way through life. I also believe that 'using them', just as when we 'Practice and Study our craft', enhances and hones those abilities.

Hopefully you can see a little easier now why a writer is so passionate about their work. Every song is truly a work of art. God gave each of us a gift and just having the chance to use it is truly a blessing.

Thank you for allowing me to share a little touch of my talents with you. I hope you were able to see a glimpse into the mindset of the Songwriter and how the process goes to pen a song. From the concept to the creation, the song is truly a manifestation of a creative idea. It is something to marvel just watching it unfold before your very eyes.

Never Underestimate The Gift !!

I hope you will never underestimate the gift you have just because you haven't used it. There is a tremendous difference between the man who can't do it and the man who just hasn't tried it yet.

Remember from my highlighted songs and stories that two local teenagers got a crack at going to Nashville. Through an unlikely turn of events, they used my dad's guitar amp. Later, Jerry House pitched Mel Tillis a song at a Guitar Pulling. Mel didn't jump for any of the songs from any of the writers there. Mel happened to get a little disgusted and asked if they had anything else.

Jerry did have something else and pitched. The song he hadn't even thought about became considered. Mel Tillis called Del Reeves, another 1960's star and charting artist. He sounded a little condescending to Mel, who turned around and cut the song anyway. The song became a hit.

Mel wrote another highlighted song that Kenny Rogers sang. Del Reeves went on to steer more into the executive end of the business who ended up helping to get signed Billy Ray Cyrus, who I highlighted in another song here.

Do you get the picture with how we start out with one thing and God changes directions? Do you see how through it all, it is our Gift that is the most unexplainable part and we can't remotely conceive of the infinite possibilities?

"It is my experience that sometimes God blesses us with something so powerful that even we don't recognize its capabilities. Just like the roots of the tree or vine, when touched by God, our efforts begin to reach out far and wide penetrating underneath the new ground out of sight yet affecting everyone who sees it (the dogwood), who feels it (the pecan), or who smells it (the honeysuckle). And, for that special one in ten thousand, he may combine the talents into an unmistakable combination… just like 'the rose'!"

~

ALL DREAMS *CAN* COME TRUE

"You got that right!" said the old gray-haired gentleman. "Now believe!"

* 9 7 9 8 4 5 5 8 2 0 3 3 5 *